ROYAL LONDON

L ondon has a charm that draws visitors from home and abroad
 are looking to explore what England's capital city has to offer. The
 fact that for hundreds of years Britain has had a Royal Family is
part of that charm, and the unique history of our monarchy forms the
basis of *Royal London*.

From palaces and parks to pomp and ceremony, from streets with royal
connections to statues commemorating past sovereigns and their
consorts, much of today's royal London is readily available to any visitor
who wishes to seek it out. But it is fascinating, too, to reflect on how parts
of London came about, thanks to those monarchs who have lived, loved,
lost and left a royal footprint. Follow in the footsteps of royalty past and
present on this journey through England's capital and beyond to Kew,
Hampton Court and Windsor.

Gill Knappett

BUCKINGHAM PALACE

In the early 17th century, James I planted 10,000 mulberry trees in a walled garden where Buckingham Palace now stands. He planned to establish a silk industry but the wrong type of mulberry tree had been chosen and the project failed.

What has become London's most famous royal residence was a much smaller property when it was built as a town house for the Duke of Buckingham in 1705. Buckingham House came into royal ownership in 1761 when George III purchased it for £28,000, renaming it the Queen's House in honour of his consort, Queen Charlotte. When she died it became known as the King's House in preparation for her son, the Prince Regent's, future role as sovereign.

By the time the Prince Regent took the throne as George IV in 1820 he had employed the architect John Nash to extend the King's House into a palace. Nash's work was a masterpiece but grand plans and spiralling costs meant the project was still unfinished by the time the king died. During the reign of his successor, William IV, another architect, Edward Blore, was employed to complete the task, although work was still taking place when King William died.

BELOW: Buckingham Palace seen from St James's Park.

RIGHT: Prince Charles, Prince Andrew, the Duchess of Cornwall, the Queen, the Duchess of Sussex, Prince Harry, Prince William and the Duchess of Cambridge on the balcony of Buckingham Palace to watch a flypast marking 100 years of the RAF in July 2018.

Soon after Queen Victoria's accession in 1837, she became the first monarch to make Buckingham Palace her home. Blore was responsible for building the balcony at Buckingham Palace and when Victoria stepped on to it to greet the crowds in celebration of the opening of the Great Exhibition in 1851, so began what is now a tradition on many royal occasions – although the now famous 'first kiss' was only established in 1981, following the marriage of Prince Charles to Lady Diana Spencer.

Today Buckingham Palace remains the official London home of the sovereign, and the Royal Standard flies when the sovereign is in residence.

The State Rooms are open to the public for ten weeks during the summer. These are lavishly decorated and furnished with priceless treasures from the Royal Collection. As the name suggests, the State Rooms are where the Queen receives guests on State occasions, but they are also used for ceremonial and other official events. Most of the 19 State Rooms were designed by John Nash and include the White Drawing Room, where members of the Royal Family gather before official events, and the Throne Room, where court ceremonies and official royal entertainment takes place.

BOTTOM: An engraving of Buckingham Palace from 1849.

ABOVE: Entrance to The Queen's Gallery, home to works of art from the Royal Collection.

Another part of Buckingham Palace which can be visited by the public at certain times of the year is **The Royal Mews**. It was George III who first decided to move his horses and carriages next to his Queen's House. Later, his son, George IV, commissioned John Nash to remodel and extend what were essentially the stables.

By the time Queen Victoria was on the throne, so many people were working at the Royal Mews that she had accommodation built on site for them, and even set up a school there for the employees' children.

BELOW: Prince Harry and Meghan Markle process through Windsor in an Ascot Landau, one of several kept at the Royal Mews, following their wedding in May 2018.

Today the Royal Mews houses all types of royal transport, including motor cars. However, it is processions with horse-drawn carriages that form a spectacular sight on royal occasions, and carriages kept here include the Diamond Jubilee State Coach, built to commemorate Queen Elizabeth II's 2012 Jubilee. But the grandest vehicle of all is the Gold State Coach. This gilded coach has been used for royal coronations ever since 1821 when it was the transport for the new king, George IV, who claimed it to be one of the most uncomfortable rides he had ever experienced.

Two types of horses are used to pull the royal carriages: Cleveland Bays and Windsor Greys, both of which are trained at the Royal Mews. Windsor Greys are known particularly for their placid temperament and are used for carriages bearing the monarch.

Also on site at Buckingham Palace is **The Queen's Gallery**, where visitors can enjoy seeing a host of changing exhibitions featuring treasures from the Royal Collection, with everything from furniture and decorative artworks to old masters and photographs on display.

The Queen's Gallery stands on an area first built as a pavilion by John Nash, and designed as an Ionic temple. It was converted into a private chapel during Queen Victoria's reign but destroyed by a bomb during the Second World War. Queen Elizabeth II recommended it become a gallery to house the Royal Collection and it opened as such in 1962. It was further expanded and modernised to mark Her Majesty's Golden Jubilee – the most important addition to Buckingham Palace for 150 years – and officially reopened in 2002.

RIGHT: Paintings by Venetian artist Canaletto on display at an exhibition in The Queen's Gallery in 2017.

ST JAMES'S PALACE

St James Hospital was an infirmary for lepers before Henry VIII built a palace on the site. Parts of the original building remain, including a gatehouse bearing the initials HA, representing King Henry and Anne Boleyn, his second wife.

Charles I spent his last night here on 29 January 1649, in order not to hear workmen erecting the scaffolding for his execution at nearby Whitehall Palace. He took Holy Communion in the Chapel Royal at St James's Palace before walking to Whitehall to meet his fate. On a happier note, several future monarchs were born at St James's Palace, including Charles II, James II and his daughters Mary II and Queen Anne.

The last monarch to reside at St James's Palace was William IV. Today it is a busy working palace and the State Apartments are often used for entertaining overseas dignitaries, although some members of the Royal Family still live at St James's Palace. Within its precincts is **York House**, where Prince Charles and his sons, Princes William and Harry, lived before they moved to **Clarence House**, also in the palace grounds, in 2003.

Prince Charles previously lived in Clarence House – a mansion built for the Duke of Clarence (later William IV) in 1825 – when his parents, Princess Elizabeth and the Duke of Edinburgh, moved there in 1949. It is where the Queen Mother moved to following her daughter's accession to the throne in 1952. When the Queen Mother died in 2002, it became the official London home of her eldest grandson, Charles. Today he and his wife, Camilla, Duchess of Cornwall, welcome guests to Clarence House in an official capacity, and for a few weeks each year the public can enjoy guided tours of parts of the house and gardens.

As the name suggests, **Spencer House**, part of the St James's Palace complex, was once owned by the ancestors of the late Diana, Princess of Wales. It was the 1st Earl Spencer who had this grand house built in the 18th century, and the family lived here until 1895. With its magnificent rooms restored to their former glory, Spencer House is open for guided tours at certain times of the year.

BELOW: **The red-brick gatehouse of St James's Palace, built 1531–36 by Henry VIII.**

WHITEHALL PALACE

All that remains of Whitehall Palace, once the largest palace in Europe, is the Banqueting House. Its beautiful ceiling, painted by Rubens – commissioned in 1630 by Charles I and glorifying his father, James I – was despised by the Parliamentarians who executed Charles here in 1649. On that bitterly cold day, he wore a thick shirt so as not to appear to shiver with fear. Eleven years later his son, Charles II, celebrated the Restoration of the Monarchy at Whitehall Palace. The building was destroyed by fire in 1698 during the reign of William III.

> Charles II died at Whitehall in 1685, famously requesting, 'Let not poor Nelly starve', a reference to his mistress Nell Gwyn.

SOMERSET HOUSE

Close to Whitehall is Somerset House, built as a palace in 1547 by Edward Seymour, first Duke of Somerset and brother of Jane Seymour (Henry VIII's third wife). It became the property of the Crown when Edward Seymour was executed for treason in 1552. James I of England's wife, Anne of Denmark, renamed it Denmark House and had it remodelled by Inigo Jones, as did Henrietta Maria of France, Charles I's consort. Its last royal resident was Catherine of Braganza, wife of Charles II, who moved out in 1693. By the time George III was on the throne it was in a state of disrepair; the original building was demolished in 1775 and a new Somerset House was built. Today the elegant Georgian building is an art centre which is open daily.

BELOW: **Somerset House** today: the original building was taken over by the Parliamentarians during the English Civil War, resuming its role as a royal residence after the Restoration.

KENSINGTON PALACE

When William III and his wife Mary II came to the throne in 1689 they commissioned Christopher Wren to convert Nottingham House, a mansion previously owned by the Earl of Nottingham, into the royal residence that became Kensington Palace.

The last reigning monarch to live at Kensington Palace was George II who died here in 1760. His great-great-granddaughter, the future Queen Victoria, was born and raised here, leading a lonely childhood almost entirely within its confines. In June 1837 the 18-year-old Princess Victoria woke to the news that her uncle, William IV, had died and she was now the sovereign. With Kensington Palace in a poor state of repair, she soon relocated to Buckingham Palace.

In recent decades the renovated Kensington Palace is where many senior royals have resided, including the Prince and Princess of Wales following their marriage in 1981. Diana, Princess of Wales continued to live here with her sons Princes William and Harry after she and Prince Charles divorced, and both William and Harry have made it their London home in adulthood. With parts of Kensington Palace open to the public, it is a popular visitor attraction all year round.

RIGHT: The King's Staircase in Kensington Palace. The 18th-century paintings by William Kent are believed to feature a number of characters from the royal household but also include the artist himself.

PALACE OF WESTMINSTER

Marshland on the banks of the River Thames outside the City walls was where in the 11th century the pious Edward the Confessor chose to build his cruciform church – Westminster Abbey – and subsequently his Palace of Westminster, better known as the Houses of Parliament. Consisting of the House of Commons and the House of Lords, it is the seat of government in the United Kingdom. Building of the tower that houses the clock generally referred to as Big Ben – one of London's most iconic landmarks – was completed in 1859. Originally called the Clock Tower, it was renamed the Elizabeth Tower in 2012 in honour of Queen Elizabeth II's Diamond Jubilee.

William the Conqueror made Westminster his main residence, as did his successors. Henry VIII was the last monarch to live here; a fire in 1512 saw him relocate to Whitehall Palace. Although the medieval Palace of Westminster endured many blazes over the centuries, one in 1834 destroyed most of the building. Subsequent rebuilding of the palace by architects Charles Barry and Augustus Pugin resulted in the magnificent Gothic masterpiece we see today.

One of the few parts to survive the 1834 fire was **Westminster Hall**, the largest banqueting hall in Europe when it was built by William Rufus,

BELOW: The Palace of Westminster's magnificent façade, seen here from the River Thames, is nearly 1,000 feet (300 metres) long.

William the Conqueror's son and heir, in 1097–99. Later monarchs improved it, including Richard II who commissioned the beautiful oak hammer-beam roof, famed for having the widest unsupported span in the country.

From 1178 until 1882 Westminster Hall became home to the main Courts of Law. Central to the English legal system it witnessed many famous trials, including that of Guy Fawkes following his failed attempt to blow up the Houses of Parliament in 1605.

LEFT: In Westminster Hall, the Duke of Edinburgh is seated next to his wife, Queen Elizabeth II, who stands to address the Houses of Parliament in 2012, her Diamond Jubilee year.

Westminster Hall has been used for the lying-in-state of sovereigns and their consorts prior to their funerals. Memorably, in 2002, following the death of the Queen Mother, 200,000 people filed past her coffin to pay their respects.

Another part of the old Palace of Westminster which survived the 19th-century inferno is the **Jewel Tower**, built in 1365–66 as a stronghold for Edward III's jewels and other royal valuables. From the 16th century it housed parliamentary records, and in the 1860s became a weights and measures office. Today, under the care of English Heritage, the Jewel Tower is a fascinating museum which is open to the public.

ABOVE: Queen Elizabeth II makes her exit following the State Opening of Parliament in 1964.

STATE OPENING OF PARLIAMENT

The memory of the Gunpowder Plot still resonates, as to this day Yeomen of the Guard carry out a ceremonial search of the cellars prior to the State Opening of Parliament by the reigning monarch.

The now televised event is one of high ceremony. The sovereign rides in a State Coach whilst the royal regalia, including the Imperial State Crown, travel in another, as the royal procession makes its way from Buckingham Palace to Westminster. On arrival the sovereign is dressed in the Robe of State and Imperial State Crown before leading the royal procession into the House of Lords for the formal Opening of Parliament.

In a ritual dating back to the time of Charles I in 1642, a House of Lords official – known as Black Rod, a reference to the ceremonial ebony stick he or she carries – summons the House of Commons. The door to the Commons is first slammed in Black Rod's face, symbolising the Commons' independence from the monarchy. Black Rod strikes the door three times, the door is opened and Members of the House of Commons make their way to the Lords Chamber.

Once the sovereign's speech has been delivered and the monarch has left, the new parliamentary year officially begins.

WESTMINSTER ABBEY

Edward the Confessor's 'west minster' (as opposed to the 'east minster', St Paul's Cathedral in the City of London) was consecrated on 28 December 1065, just days before he died. Edward – the only English monarch to be canonised – is enshrined here. His was to be the first of a long tradition of royal burials and memorials at the abbey: Elizabeth I and her half-sister, Mary I, share a tomb, although only Elizabeth's effigy, carved in white marble, is seen; a more elaborate, canopied resting place belongs to her cousin, Mary Queen of Scots.

Another tradition began on Christmas Day 1066, when William I, victorious at the Battle of Hastings, was crowned here. Westminster Abbey has been the site for coronations of English monarchs ever since.

In 1245 Henry III began rebuilding the abbey, and the English Gothic building that stands today remains much as he intended, its style influenced by the opulent French cathedrals he favoured. The nave alone – the highest in England – took 150 years to complete.

Westminster Abbey remains a place of regular worship and has been the venue for several royal weddings, amongst them Prince Albert (later George VI) to Elizabeth Bowes-Lyon in 1923, and both their daughters: Princess Elizabeth (Queen Elizabeth II) in 1947 and Princess Margaret in 1960. More recently, the Queen's grandson Prince William married Catherine Middleton here in 2011.

BELOW: Westminster Abbey at night. Within its walls are some of the finest examples of medieval architecture in London.

ROYAL PECULIARS

Westminster Abbey is known as a Royal Peculiar, which means it falls under the jurisdiction of the monarch rather than a bishop, a concept that dates back to Anglo-Saxon times. Other Royal Peculiars in central London are: the Chapel Royal and Queen's Chapel in St James's Palace; the Chapels of St John the Evangelist and St Peter ad Vincula in the Tower of London; the Queen's Chapel of the Savoy, a private chapel governed by the Duchy of Lancaster and situated next to the Savoy Hotel in the Strand; the Chapel of St Mary Undercroft in the Palace of Westminster; and the Royal Foundation of St Katharine, founded in 1147 by Queen Matilda, wife of King Stephen, as a church and hospital next to the Tower of London.

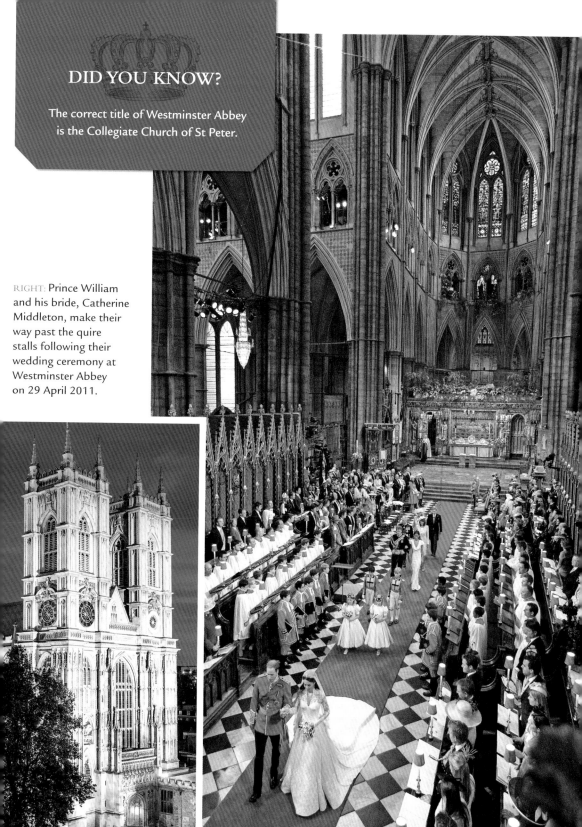

RIGHT: Prince William and his bride, Catherine Middleton, make their way past the quire stalls following their wedding ceremony at Westminster Abbey on 29 April 2011.

CORONATIONS

Coronations have been central to the story of Westminster Abbey since 1066. That first coronation ceremony was memorable ... but not necessarily for the right reasons. Shouts of acclaim from William the Conqueror's English guests were misinterpreted by the French-speaking guards as a protest, and they set fire to nearby houses in retaliation. Although the ceremony continued, panicked guests left the abbey, the clergy were terrified and King William 'was trembling violently'.

The Coronation Chair has formed part of the ceremony since it was first used by Edward II in 1308. It was made on the order of his father,

LEFT: Spectators in grandstands watch as King George V and Queen Mary, in the Gold State Coach, approach Westminster Abbey for His Majesty's Coronation, 22 June 1911. More than 50 such grandstands were erected along the processional route.

RIGHT: Queen Elizabeth II at her Coronation in Westminster Abbey, 2 June 1953. As for her wedding gown six years earlier, the Queen's Coronation dress, embroidered with the emblems of the United Kingdom and the Commonwealth, was the work of British fashion designer Norman Hartnell.

Edward I, to enclose the Stone of Scone, claimed by the latter in 1296 after his invasion of Scotland. Many Scottish kings had been crowned on the legendary Stone of Scone, which was finally returned to Scotland in 1996.

In nearly 1,000 years of history at Westminster Abbey there have been three sovereigns who were never crowned: Edward V who became king at the age of 12 in 1483 but disappeared, most likely murdered; Lady Jane Grey who was deposed after just nine days as queen in 1553; and Edward VIII who abdicated in December 1936, five months before his planned coronation. Instead his brother, George VI, was crowned at the coronation ceremony on 12 May 1937.

However, what many people today recall is 2 June 1953, his daughter Queen Elizabeth II's coronation day. It was the first time such an event had been televised, and many families purchased their first television set for the occasion. Following months of preparation, Queen Elizabeth II, dressed in a gown by Norman Hartnell and accompanied by six maids of honour, took centre stage. Under the guidance of the Archbishop of Canterbury, Geoffrey Fisher, she undertook six symbolic stages of historic ritual: the **Recognition**, during which, having arrived in the coronation 'theatre' she was presented to the congregation; the **Oath**, a promise to govern with justice and mercy, and to maintain the Protestant religion; the **Consecration**, the most solemn part of the service, for which the Queen was hidden from view and dressed in a simple white robe; next the **Investiture** with the presentation of the Coronation Regalia – Spurs and the Jewelled Sword of Offering, the Armills, the Royal Robe with the Stole Royal, the Orb, Rings and two Sceptres, followed by the crowning with the Crown of St Edward; and the **Enthronement**, when the newly crowned monarch ascended the throne for the first time to receive the **Homage**, first from the Archbishop of Canterbury, then her husband, the Duke of Edinburgh, before the rest of the clergy and peers vowed their loyalty.

ST PAUL'S CATHEDRAL

Since AD 604 a place of Christian worship dedicated to one saint has stood on the site today occupied by the architectural masterpiece that is St Paul's Cathedral. It was following the Great Fire of London of 1666, which destroyed the third St Paul's, that architect Christopher Wren was given a royal warrant to rebuild the cathedral, completed in 1711 during the reign of Queen Anne. Even today, nestled amongst striking modern buildings, its iconic dome still dominates the City of London skyline.

St Paul's Cathedral has been the venue for many royal events, in particular celebrations. It was here in 1415 that Henry V prayed before he departed for France, and where, following his victory at the Battle of Agincourt, a thanksgiving service was held. In 1501 Prince Arthur, eldest son of Henry VII, married Catherine of Aragon at St Paul's. It was a lavish occasion, the interior of the cathedral redesigned for the ceremony, the bride and groom both dressed in white satin, and the public treated to an endless supply of wine at the west door. Over 400 years later, in 1981, it is where Prince Charles and Lady Diana Spencer were married, chosen over the smaller Westminster Abbey because of the number of guests attending this state occasion.

An inscription on the paving outside the cathedral commemorates Queen Victoria's Diamond Jubilee in 1897; the celebration service took place on the steps of St Paul's as Victoria was too frail to alight her carriage and climb the steps.

BELOW: St Paul's Cathedral in the heart of the City of London.

CITY OF LONDON

At London Wall in the City of London – the oldest part of England's capital – is the Museum of London, which presents a fascinating history from the earliest times to the present day. The 'Square Mile' that is the City is where the Romans built their settlement, destroyed by Boudicca, Queen of the Iceni, c. AD 60. In 1215, King John, of Magna Carta fame, granted the City a charter to elect its own mayor, and within its boundaries only the monarch takes precedence over the Lord Mayor of the City of London. Once a highly populated residential area, since the 19th century it has been best-known as a financial district and business centre.

BELOW: Crowds line the streets for Queen Victoria's Diamond Jubilee ceremony at St Paul's Cathedral in 1897.

TOWER OF LONDON

Although many much taller buildings in the City of London now tower over the Tower of London, when its White Tower was built by William the Conqueror in the 11th century it was an imposing edifice on the banks of the Thames. Many of his successors added to the complex over the centuries.

As well as being a one-time royal residence, the Tower of London has also housed the Royal Mint and is still home to the **Crown Jewels**, which comprise the regalia used on ceremonial occasions, most significantly at a coronation. Most of the items date from the reign of Charles II; the Parliamentarians destroyed the Crown Jewels following the execution of Charles I, so new regalia was made for Charles II's coronation in 1661. Previous to that, legend has it that King John lost some of the Crown Jewels in the Wash off the coast of East Anglia in 1216.

Many people, kings and queens amongst them, have been imprisoned in the Tower of London, including, from 1465, Henry VI during the Wars of the Roses. Although he was re-crowned in 1470, he died at the Tower

The Queen with Yeomen of the Guard at the Tower of London in 2004.

BELOW: **The Tower of London, now a World Heritage Site.**

BELOW RIGHT: **The Imperial State Crown,** one of the highlights of the Crown Jewels, being carried to the annual State Opening of Parliament.

the following year, likely murdered while at prayer on the orders of his successor, Edward IV. Each year the anniversary of Henry VI's death is marked with the Ceremony of the Lilies and the Roses, with flowers laid by students from Eton College and King's College, Cambridge, both establishments founded by the monarch. Perhaps the most famous prisoners of all, however, were the Princes in the Tower: the remains of two boys discovered in 1674 are thought to have been the 12-year-old Edward V and his younger brother, their mysterious disappearance generally attributed to their uncle, Richard of Gloucester, crowned Richard III in 1483.

Lady Jane Grey, the nine-day queen ousted by Mary I, was incarcerated here before being executed for high treason on Tower Green in 1554. Two of Henry VIII's wives had previously met the same fate: Anne Boleyn and Catherine Howard. The last beheading on Tower Green came in 1601 when Robert Devereux, Earl of Sussex, fell out of favour with Elizabeth I, although the final beheading on Tower Hill came much later, in 1747, when Simon Fraser, Lord Lovat, was condemned for supporting Bonnie Prince Charlie's attempt to regain the British throne.

Two of the most popular sights for today's visitors are the ravens and uniformed Yeoman Warders who both protect the Tower of London. The ravens may do so by legend alone, but Yeoman Warders end each day by locking up with the ancient Ceremony of the Keys.

Royal Ceremonials

CHANGING THE GUARD

One of London's most-watched ceremonies is Changing the Guard, more properly known as the Guard Mounting, which takes place at Buckingham Palace. The colourful 45-minute ceremony, to the accompaniment of a military band, is carried out by soldiers of the Foot Guards who have protected the monarch and royal palaces since 1660. At the given time the Old Guard, dressed in traditional red tunics and bearskin hats, goes off duty and hands over to the New Guard from the nearby Wellington Barracks.

LEFT: A military band marches past the Victoria Memorial outside Buckingham Palace as part of the Changing the Guard ceremony.

TROOPING THE COLOUR

S ince 1748 the sovereign's official birthday has been celebrated in the summer months, with the hope of fine weather, and today is always held in June. The Birthday Parade, or Trooping the Colour, is an elaborate pageant with its roots in the military tradition of parading (trooping) the flags (colours) of a battalion so that its soldiers could easily recognise them on the battlefield.

Since 1987 the Queen has attended the Trooping the Colour ceremony in a carriage, but prior to that she rode her own horse, seated side-saddle and dressed in uniform. The procession starts at Buckingham Palace and Her Majesty is escorted by the mounted Household Cavalry down The Mall to Horse Guards Parade, where over 1,400 soldiers, accompanied by the massed military bands of the Household Division, are on parade. Here the Queen receives the royal salute and inspects her troops. Each year one of five regiments of the Foot Guards is chosen to parade their regimental colours. The Foot Guards, Household Cavalry and the King's Troop, Royal Horse Artillery all parade past the Queen before she returns to Buckingham Palace, where she and other members of the Royal Family step out onto the balcony to see a fly-past by the Royal Air Force.

BELOW: **King George V and his cousin Prince Arthur of Connaught ride to the Trooping the Colour ceremony in 1912. Over 100 years later (inset), his granddaughter Queen Elizabeth II attends the ceremony with the Duke of Edinburgh in 2017.**

HORSE GUARDS PARADE

This military parade ground that is the venue for the annual Trooping the Colour ceremony was once the tiltyard of Whitehall Palace, where Henry VIII enjoyed jousting. Another reminder of an earlier monarch at Horse Guards is the black mark above the figure two on the clock face that marks the time at which Charles I was executed in 1649 at Banqueting House on the opposite side of the road.

Horse Guards is named after the troops who have performed a ceremony here ever since the Restoration of the Monarchy in 1660. The daily Changing the Queen's Life Guard sees the changeover of the Old Guard to the New Guard, members of the mounted Household Cavalry, made up of the Life Guard and the Blues and Royals. The New Guard, dressed in their colourful uniforms and plumed helmets, are a spectacular sight as they ride their immaculately turned-out horses through London from Hyde Park Barracks to Horse Guards for the ceremony.

BELOW: The Glass Coach carries Princess Margaret across Horse Guards Parade as she makes her way to Westminster Abbey for her wedding to Anthony Armstrong-Jones in May 1960.

BEATING THE RETREAT

A precursor to Trooping the Colour is Beating the Retreat, a pageant which takes place at Horse Guards Parade on two consecutive evenings in June. The ceremony's origins date back to days of warfare when drums were beaten to signal the end of the day's fighting, and troops returned to camp and mounted the guard for the night.

LEFT: The Dismounting Ceremony at Horse Guards Parade.

BELOW: The Royal Marines Band rehearsing for Beating the Retreat at Horse Guards Parade.

HOUSEHOLD CAVALRY

The Sovereign is head of the British Armed Forces, officially called Her Majesty's Armed Forces. The Household Division headquarters at Whitehall is responsible for State ceremonial and public duties in both London and Windsor, and consists of the Household Cavalry and Foot Guards of which Her Majesty is Colonel-in-Chief.

The Household Cavalry Mounted Regiment is based in London's Hyde Park Barracks. The regiment has two sections: the **Life Guards**, formed in 1660 by the men who had guarded Charles II during his exile, and the **Blues and Royals**. The latter was formed in 1969 when the Royal Horse Guards (the Blues) and the Royal Dragoons (the Royals) were amalgamated. The Blues were originally raised on the order of Oliver Cromwell in 1650, and subsequently re-raised by Charles II who in 1661 created what became the British Army. The Royals also originated with the Parliamentarians and became known as the Tangier Horse before being acquired by Charles II on his marriage to his Portuguese wife, Catherine of Braganza.

BELOW: **An illustration showing Queen Victoria and Prince Albert inspecting wounded soldiers of the Grenadier Guards at Buckingham Palace, 1855.**

FOOT GUARDS

The Foot Guards, who amongst other duties perform Changing the Guard at Buckingham Palace, consists of five regiments, one of which is chosen to display its colours before the sovereign at Trooping the Colour.

Like the Life Guards, the **Grenadier Guards** was formed out of the bodyguard of the exiled Charles II, and founded in 1856 in Flanders. It is the British Army's most senior infantry, although the honour of being the most senior regiment overall belongs to the Life Guards. The **Coldstream Guards**, founded in 1650 by the Parliamentarians, subsequently entered the service of the Crown and claims the title of being the oldest regiment in continuous service in the British Army. Unlike many of the other regiments which were formed by Charles II, it was his father, Charles I, on whose orders the **Scots Guards** were founded in 1642. The **Irish Guards** came into being on 1 April 1900 by order of Queen Victoria, commemorating the Irishmen who fought for the British Empire in the Second Boer War. The most recent regiment of Foot Guards is the **Welsh Guards**, raised by order of George V in 1915.

BELOW: The Queen is Colonel-in-Chief of the Grenadier Guards, and is seen here with them in 2013.

KINGS TROOP, ROYAL HORSE ARTILLERY

After the Second World War, when horse-drawn artillery was no longer used, this ceremonial unit was formed at the request of George VI so that a horse artillery could be used for State ceremonies. What had been the Riding Troop became the Royal Horse Artillery in 1946, with the King's Troop added to its name the following year. When she acceded to the throne, Queen Elizabeth II retained the name in her father's honour. Their duties include firing gun salutes from Hyde Park, Green Park and the Tower of London on special anniversaries and occasions, including royal births.

THE ROYAL TOURNAMENT

The Royal Tournament was the world's largest military tattoo, held annually by the British Armed Forces from 1880 to 1999, latterly at Earl's Court. Along with military bands and re-enactments, a popular aspect of the event was the musical drive, performed from 1947 by the King's Troop, Royal Horse Artillery.

ROYAL PROCLAMATIONS

One of the most memorable royal proclamations occurs when a new monarch succeeds to the throne on the death of the reigning king or queen. Customarily, the Accession Council meets at St James's Palace, and the new sovereign holds a first Council and reads out the Oath. A principal proclamation is made from a balcony at St James's Palace, accompanied by a gun salute, after which heralds proceed to other locations in London, amongst them the original site of Temple Bar and the Royal Exchange.

Temple Bar, marking the boundary between the City of London and Westminster, was once a simple chain between wooden posts, later replaced by a wooden gatehouse with a prison above it, which in turn was replaced in the 17th century by a much grander structure designed by Christopher Wren. By 1878 an increasing number of horse-drawn carriages trying to pass through its archway were causing congestion, so it was dismantled and relocated to an estate in Hertfordshire. However, in 2004 Temple Bar returned to London and is now situated at Paternoster Square, close to St Paul's Cathedral.

It was to St Paul's that Elizabeth I was processing in 1588 for a thanksgiving service following the defeat of the Spanish Armada when she rode through Temple Bar to be met by the Lord Mayor of London. He presented her with the keys to the City, and she handed him a jewelled sword. Thus began a tradition that has been followed for centuries on certain royal occasions, including in 2012 when Queen Elizabeth II entered the City for a national service of thanksgiving for her Diamond Jubilee. Although she did not stop at the original site of Temple Bar, she was met on the steps of St Paul's Cathedral by the Lord Mayor and touched the pearl-encrusted sword which he presented to her as a sign of his loyalty. He then carried the sword as he processed before the Queen into the cathedral, indicating that the sovereign was

RIGHT: The Lord Mayor of London leads Queen Elizabeth II into St Paul's Cathedral for the service of thanksgiving for Her Majesty's Diamond Jubilee in 2012.

BELOW: Old Temple Bar, now situated at Paternoster Square, is the only surviving gateway to the City of London.

ABOVE: **The Royal Exchange** (left), at the heart of busy Bank Junction, *c.*1912.

under his protection while within the City.

The first building on the site of the **Royal Exchange** in the City was originally a trading centre simply called the Exchange, established by merchant Sir Thomas Gresham in 1566. When it was officially opened by Elizabeth I in 1571 she gave it its royal status. By 1660 additional floors had been added for retail, reflected in its 21st-century reincarnation as a luxurious shopping centre. That first building was destroyed by the Great Fire of London; its replacement also fell victim to fire in 1838, and the current building was opened by Queen Victoria in 1844.

VICTORIA & ALBERT'S LONDON

One of the greatest royal love matches of all time was that of Queen Victoria and her consort, Prince Albert. The English princess, born at Kensington Palace in 1819, and the German prince were cousins, and first met when Victoria was 16. At their second meeting in 1839 she, by now Queen Victoria, proposed to him and they married the following year in the Chapel Royal, St James's Palace. There are many aspects of London which honour the pair.

Albert was a man of integrity who supported public causes. The peak of his success in Britain was the **Great Exhibition of 1851**, held in Hyde Park in the purpose-built Crystal Palace – a huge structure which was tested for its strength prior to the opening by soldiers marching and jumping on the floors.

Following the success of the Great Exhibition, which had brought together exhibits from all over the world and attracted over 6 million visitors, Albert wanted to use some of the profits to build museums, schools, colleges and a concert hall. The concert hall, to be called the Hall of Arts and Science, had not been started by the time Albert died from typhoid in 1861; in 1867 his widow laid the foundation stone and announced that the building would be called the **Royal Albert Hall**.

OPPOSITE: The Queen visits the 'Victorian Vision' exhibition at the Victoria & Albert Museum in 2001.

BELOW: The Crystal Palace, erected in Hyde Park for the Great Exhibition of 1851.

BELOW: **The ornate Albert Memorial, unveiled in 1872, depicts Prince Albert holding the catalogue of his Great Exhibition.**

Another project proposed by Albert following the Great Exhibition was a museum dedicated to art and design from around the world. Originally founded in 1852, a new building was eventually commissioned and named the **Victoria & Albert Museum** when Queen Victoria laid the foundation stone in 1899, one of the last major public events the 80-year-old sovereign ever attended.

Opposite the Royal Albert Hall is the **Albert Memorial**. So impressed was Queen Victoria when she first saw it that she knighted its designer, George Gilbert Scott. In 1915 the elaborately decorated monument was painted black to prevent it attracting attention from the enemy during the First World War, and it was not until 1998 that it was re-gilded.

Despite there being seven assassination attempts on Queen Victoria's life during her 63 years on the throne – her long reign only topped by Queen Elizabeth II in 2015 – she lived to the age of 81. Like Albert, Victoria has her share of monuments in London, the most impressive being the **Victoria Memorial** which stands outside Buckingham Palace, looking along The Mall towards **Admiralty Arch**. The idea for both the Victoria Memorial and Admiralty Arch to commemorate the queen was that of her son Edward VII, although he died before either structure was completed.

ROYAL STREETS & STATUES

Many parts of London have royal connections, including streets and establishments named after royalty, and areas of the capital adorned with royal statues.

Amongst them is **The Mall**, leading from Buckingham Palace to Admiralty Arch. The Mall, like the nearby Pall Mall, takes its name from the game of *paille maille*, similar to croquet and popular during the reign of Charles II. Along The Mall are memorials to Queen Elizabeth II's parents: George VI's statue was erected in 1955 and alongside it, flanked by bronze depictions of scenes from the Second World War, stands his wife. At the unveiling ceremony in 2009, Prince Charles said, 'At long last my grandparents are reunited in this joint symbol, which in particular reminds us of all they stood for and meant to so many during the darkest days this country has ever faced.'

Now headquarters of The Commonwealth of Nations, the 18th-century **Marlborough House** was built on land once used as a pheasantry for St James's Palace. There are memorials to two dowager queens who resided here after they were widowed: Queen Mary, who lived here from 1936; and Queen Alexandra, whose grand statue, unveiled in 1932, seven years after her death, symbolises her virtues of Faith, Hope and Love.

Kings Road, Chelsea was laid in the 17th century for the monarch to travel between Whitehall Palace and Hampton Court, and later Kew, to avoid London's congested streets. Other than royalty, those with a copper token stamped 'The King's Private Roads' were also permitted to use it.

LEFT: Queen Elizabeth II rides along The Mall from Buckingham Palace in the Gold State Coach on her way to St Paul's Cathedral for a service of thanksgiving to celebrate her Golden Jubilee in 2002.

ABOVE RIGHT: Grinling Gibbons' gilded statue of Charles II dressed as a Roman Emperor stands in Figure Court at the Royal Hospital Chelsea.

BELOW: This memorial by sculptor Sir Alfred Gilbert to Queen Alexandra, wife of Edward VII, is set into a garden wall at Marlborough House.

A statue of Charles II stands in the grounds of the **Royal Hospital Chelsea**, for it was he who commissioned the building of this retirement home for soldiers in the 17th century. It still serves that purpose to this day and the 'Chelsea Pensioners' are a familiar sight in London in their traditional scarlet uniform when representing the hospital at special events and parades.

Other hospitals with royal connections include the **Royal London Hospital** at Whitechapel, founded as the London Infirmary and renamed in 1990 when Queen Elizabeth II visited to commemorate its 250th anniversary. At the hospital is a statue of Queen Alexandra 'who in 1900 introduced to England the Finsen Light Cure for lupus'. **King's College Hospital** was established in 1840 as a training hospital for the university given royal charter by George IV in 1829; in 1909 the hospital moved to its current location in **Denmark Hill**, named for Queen Anne's consort, George of Denmark. Prince Charles' wife, Camilla, Duchess of Cornwall, was born at King's College Hospital in 1947.

Several London theatres owe their names to royalty, including the West End's **Prince Edward Theatre**, built in 1930 and named after the future King Edward VIII. **The Old Vic** – its popular name since the 19th century – in south-east London was originally the Royal Coburg Theatre, its patron being Prince Leopold of Coburg, son-in-law of George IV. Its name changed to the Royal Victoria Theatre in 1833 in honour of the future queen, and it became a popular venue for Victorian music-hall entertainment.

Royal Parks

ST JAMES'S PARK

L ondon's extensive open green spaces owned by the Crown
are managed by The Royal Parks, a charity launched in 2017.
Amongst the eight parks under its care are those in central
London: St James's Park, Green Park, Hyde Park, Kensington Gardens
and Regent's Park.

Both Buckingham Palace and St James's Palace look out over
St James's Park, London's oldest royal park. What was once marshland
was drained by Henry VIII for use as a hunting ground, and is where
James I created a formal garden with a menagerie that included crocodiles.
The public were first admitted to the park during the reign of Charles II,
who landscaped the grounds and merged several small ponds to form a
canal in which he occasionally swam. Pelicans are a feature of St James's
Park, first introduced here when the Russian ambassador gifted a pair to
Charles II. He was very fond of birds and installed an aviary on the
southern edge of the park, now known as Birdcage Walk.

GREEN PARK

The triangular Green Park is bordered
by Piccadilly, Queen's Walk and
Constitution Hill, which is where a
would-be assassin fired two shots at
Queen Victoria in 1840.

The park was once a graveyard
adjoining the hospital where St
James's Palace now stands,
transformed with walkways for
public use by Charles II in the 17th
century. Rumour has it that his wife,
Catherine of Braganza, had all the
flowers removed from the park when
she found him picking blooms for his
mistress, and there are still no formal
flowerbeds here to this day.

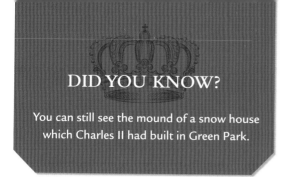
HYDE PARK

The largest of London's royal parks at 350 acres
(140 ha), what was once the manor of Hyde
belonged to Westminster Abbey before being
seized by Henry VIII. Today Hyde Park is popular
with walkers, joggers, cyclists, horse riders,
tennis players and boaters but in previous
centuries it was used as a royal hunting ground,
for duels ... and by highwaymen. William III
feared them as he walked in the dark along
Rotten Row, the route from Kensington Palace
to St James's Palace, so had oil lamps suspended
from the trees, making it the first road in
England to be lit at night.

It was James I who, in the early 17th century,
first opened Hyde Park to the public. Its famous
lake, the Serpentine, was created by George II's
wife, Caroline, who had the flow of the
Westbourne River dammed in 1730. Skaters
took to the Serpentine when it froze in the hard winters of 1767 and 1784,
and the hardy Serpentine Swimming Club has taken to its icy waters every
Christmas Day since 1864. In recent years an ice rink has been installed in
the park in the lead up to Christmas as part of the festive Winter
Wonderland. And continuing the watery theme, visitors to the park love to
dip their toes in the Princess Diana Memorial Fountain, created in her
memory in 2004.

Close to Hyde Park Corner, once the site of a toll gate for people
entering London, is the ornate Queen Elizabeth Gate, unveiled in 1991
and celebrating the Queen Mother. Also nearby stands Wellington Arch,
commissioned by George IV in 1825 as an entrance to Buckingham Palace
and moved to its present position in 1882. Close to Speaker's Corner in
Hyde Park is Marble Arch, designed as the main entrance to Buckingham
Palace but deemed too small and moved to its new position in 1851, prior
to the Great Exhibition taking place in Hyde Park.

ABOVE: The Princess
Diana Memorial
Fountain in Hyde Park.

OPPOSITE: An artist's
impression of a view of
St James's Park from
Green Park, c.1820.

KENSINGTON GARDENS

A vestige of the Great Exhibition of 1851 is Alexandra Gate, situated between Hyde Park and Kensington Gardens.

Kensington Gardens were once part of Hyde Park and the former grounds of Kensington Palace. George II first opened the park to the public but only on Saturdays and only admitting 'respectably dressed people'. It was William IV who opened the park all year round.

Hyde Park's Serpentine becomes the Long Water in Kensington Gardens, and near its bank stands a statue of J.M. Barrie's fictional character Peter Pan, much loved by children. Also loved by children is the playground dedicated to Diana, Princess of Wales, where there is lots to explore, including a sensory trail and pirate ship.

The **Serpentine Gallery** in Kensington Gardens has been exhibiting artworks since 1970, whilst the **Serpentine Sackler Gallery**, on the Hyde Park side of Serpentine Bridge, opened in 2013.

BELOW: Marking two decades since the death of Diana, Princess of Wales, the White Garden at Kensington Palace was opened in 2017 in celebration of her life. It was in the White Garden later that year that Prince Harry and Meghan Markle formally announced their engagement.

REGENT'S PARK

Named for the Prince Regent, later George IV, Regent's Park is renowned for its tree-lined pathways and formal gardens, but also has four children's playgrounds and is where London Zoo is located.

This park lies on land once belonging to the Abbess of Barking before Henry VIII claimed it as another hunting ground, known as Marylebone Park. Like some of the other royal parks, the land was later sold by the Parliamentarians. By the time Charles II returned from exile, thousands of its ancient trees had been cut down and it became farmland until its potential for something grander was realised.

The land was enclosed as a park in 1812 and John Nash was commissioned to develop it. He envisaged it as a setting for a palace for the Prince Regent and 56 classically designed villas. In the event the palace did not materialise and only eight villas were built, although more Nash-designed terraces were erected around the edges of the park. Cumberland Terrace is one such row of houses, named for Ernest, Duke of Cumberland, younger brother of George IV. A flat here was once home to Mrs Simpson and frequently visited by Edward VIII. When news of his abdication broke, angry crowds gathered outside and Mrs Simpson fled to France to await her divorce, eventually marrying the man who gave up the royal Crown for love.

BELOW: This unusual photograph of Regent's Park shows a camel being used to help mow the lawns in 1911. London Zoo, situated in the park, opened to the public in 1847 and for some years camel rides were one of the attractions.

ROYAL GREENWICH

Five miles east of the City of London and situated on the River Thames lies the **Royal Borough of Greenwich**, a World Heritage Site granted the title 'Royal Borough' in 2012 in celebration of Queen Elizabeth II's Diamond Jubilee. However, it has had royal links for hundreds of years, ever since Henry V's brother Humphrey, Duke of Gloucester was permitted to enclose the manor of Greenwich to create a park in the early 15th century.

The Duke's manor house, Bella Court, was remodelled and renamed the Palace of Placentia (Palace of Pleasures). It was the birthplace of Henry VIII, who married three of his wives there: Catherine of Aragon, Anne Boleyn and Anne of Cleves. Henry's daughters, Mary I and Queen Elizabeth I, were also born at the Palace, and his only son, 15-year-old Edward VI, died there.

James I's wife, Anne of Denmark, employed Inigo Jones to design a house at Greenwich 'fit for a queen'. The **Queen's House** was finally completed in 1637 by Henrietta Maria, wife of Charles I, who called it her 'house of delights'. During the Civil War of 1642–49 the Queen's House was used by the Parliamentarians; it later become a biscuit factory and, in the 19th century, a school for sailors' children. However, it was eventually

BELOW: **In splendid symmetry: view from the Old Royal Naval College to the Queen's House.**

restored to its former glory and opened by George VI in 1937 as part of the **National Maritime Museum**, celebrating Britain's seafaring heritage.

After the Restoration, Charles II re-landscaped the park, had Placentia Palace pulled down and planned to replace it with a Wren-designed building. After Charles' death, William and Mary later demolished what he had started and commissioned instead the Royal Hospital for Seamen, again to Wren's design and considered one of England's finest classical buildings. In 1873 it became the Royal Naval College; its beautiful Painted Hall by Sir James Thornhill and the grounds of what is now known as the **Old Royal Naval College** are open to the public.

Set on a hill, **Greenwich Park**'s 183 acres (74 ha) offers panoramic views across the Thames and London. Amongst its many attractions is the **Royal Observatory**. In 1675 Charles II had appointed the first Astronomer Royal, John Flamsteed, after whom the original building, Flamsteed House, is named. Since 1854 the Royal Observatory at Greenwich has been famed as the home of Greenwich Mean Time, the basis for time measurement for most of the world. The Royal Observatory as a scientific centre, however, moved out of London in the 1950s due to problems with light pollution. The Royal Observatory at Greenwich now forms part of the National Maritime Museum and is where visitors can enjoy exploring time and space, including at its London Planetarium.

BELOW: The Painted Hall at the Old Royal Naval College.

BELOW RIGHT: King George V and Queen Mary in the grounds of the Royal Observatory during a visit to Greenwich in 1925.

ROYAL BOTANIC GARDENS & PALACE, KEW

Just eight miles from central London is Kew, popular in royal circles in medieval times because of its proximity to Richmond where a royal manor was established, and where, in 1501, Richmond Palace was built.

Kew's **Royal Botanic Gardens** were once private gardens belonging to Frederick, Prince of Wales, heir to George II. Frederick and his wife, Princess Augusta, lived in the White House in the grounds from 1731, and he introduced the plants and trees that formed the basis for the now world-renowned collection. When Frederick died in 1751, nine years before his father, his widow continued to work on landscaping and introducing more species of plants, today the most diverse collection in the world.

COMMEMORATING THE PRINCESS OF WALES

Princess Augusta's work at Kew was commemorated by one of her successors to the title Princess of Wales when Princess Diana opened the Princess of Wales Conservatory in 1987. Exotic plants from ten different climate zones are grown in the conservatory.

BELOW: The Palm House at Kew, constructed in 1844 to house tropical plants brought back to the UK by Victorian explorers.

Kew Palace, originally known as the Dutch Houses, has stood in the grounds at Kew since it was built in 1631 for a Flemish merchant. It was leased to George II and Queen Caroline as a country retreat, and their grandson, George III, later purchased the property. George III and his wife, Queen Charlotte, used it as a royal nursery for their 15 children. After Queen Charlotte's death in 1818 Kew Palace stood empty until the Royal Botanic Gardens acquired it in 1896. It opened to the public, by permission of Queen Victoria, in 1899.

ABOVE: Queen Elizabeth II at the Royal Botanical Gardens, Kew in 2004, when she unveiled a plaque commemorating it as a World Heritage Site.

Queen Charlotte's Cottage, now also open to the public, was built in 1770 as a royal 'rustic retreat', and overlooked a menagerie where kangaroos were kept, some of the first in Britain. In 1818 the cottage was the venue for celebrations following the double wedding at Kew Palace of George III's sons, William, Duke of Clarence (later William IV) and Edward, Duke of Kent. When their elder brother, George IV, died in 1830, without a legitimate child surviving to succeed him, an heir of William IV was expected to eventually take the throne. However, none of William's legitimate children survived him either and it was Edward, Duke of Kent's only child, Victoria, who became the next monarch.

RIGHT: Kew Palace. Today visitors can see Queen Charlotte's bedroom, which remains, at her granddaughter Queen Victoria's request, as it was when her grandmother lived there.

HAMPTON COURT PALACE

T he building of Hampton Court as a palace for Cardinal Thomas Wolsey began in 1514. In 1528, unable to persuade the Pope to allow Henry VIII to divorce Catherine of Aragon, Wolsey fell out of favour with the monarch, who took Hampton Court for himself and made it a royal palace.

The Tudor king rebuilt and extended the palace and it became a favoured retreat and place of power, just 12 miles upriver from the centre of London.

Oliver Cromwell lived in unaccustomed luxury at Hampton Court during the English Civil War, but it became a royal palace once again after the Restoration.

When William and Mary succeeded to the throne in 1689, they employed architect Christopher Wren to modernise Hampton Court Palace. However, much of Henry VIII's Tudor palace still remains, including the Great Hall with its stunning hammer-beam roof and stained-glass window featuring Henry and the coats of arms of his six wives, and the colourful Chapel Royal with its opulent vaulted ceiling.

BELOW: The Great Gatehouse at Hampton Court Palace. It was at Hampton Court that Jane Seymour, Henry VIII's third wife, gave birth to his son and heir, Edward VI.

The grounds at Hampton Court were also developed by its royal residents. The Privy Garden provided a private refuge for Henry VIII but today's formal layout is a reconstruction of William III's 1701 design. William and Mary's Great Fountain Garden, where yew trees planted during their reign still stand, provides a splendid view from the Queen's Drawing Room, lavishly decorated by their successor, Queen Anne.

The famous Hampton Court Maze is thought to have been completed during Queen Anne's reign, and has been one of the most popular attractions for visitors here since Queen Victoria opened the palace and gardens to the public in 1838.

The last sovereign to live at Hampton Court was George II; his wife, Queen Caroline, commissioned William Kent to paint the intricate artwork on the walls and ceiling of the Queen's Staircase. George II brought his family and court here each summer until Queen Caroline died in 1737. The building was then used as 'grace and favour apartments' until the 1960s, but is today one of England's most popular visitor attractions under the care of Historic Royal Palaces.

BELOW: The Great Hall, built for Henry VIII at Hampton Court Palace. Here in 1603 William Shakespeare's company of actors, the King's Men, first performed *Hamlet* and *Macbeth* for King James I.

THE MAGIC GARDEN

Seen here being opened by the Duchess of Cambridge in 2016, the Magic Garden is an enchanting children's play area and garden, built on the site of Henry VIII's tiltyard used for jousting tournaments. Each part of the garden represents myths and legends, and there is even a huge smoke-breathing dragon.

WINDSOR CASTLE

S ituated just over 20 miles from London on high ground overlooking the River Thames is Windsor Castle. It was started by William the Conqueror in 1070 and today is the largest occupied castle in the world.

William I's fortress was not a royal residence until the reign of Henry I. His grandson, Henry II, replaced timber walls with stone and extended it into a palace in the 12th century, with a Lower Ward and an Upper Ward, and the landmark Round Tower replacing a Norman keep. More rebuilding was carried out by Henry III, and his great-grandson Edward III further expanded the castle into an impressive royal dwelling.

Improvements, extensions and modernisations took place during the reigns of later monarchs: Elizabeth I built a gallery, now part of the Royal Library; Charles II's grand State Apartments remained virtually unchanged for over 100 years; George III introduced many internal improvements and transformed the exterior of the castle to make it even more imposing; and George IV's additions included the Waterloo Chamber, lined with portraits including those from the military who were victorious at the Battle of Waterloo. During Queen Victoria's reign the State Apartments were opened to the public for the first time.

OPPOSITE: On her 90th birthday in 2016, Queen Elizabeth II and the Duke of Edinburgh stand in an open-top car as they are driven through the streets of Windsor, greeted by crowds of well-wishers.

BELOW: Prince Harry and Meghan Markle ride in their carriage through the grounds of Windsor Castle after their wedding ceremony at St George's Chapel, 19 May 2018.

In the Second World War, Windsor Castle was considered a safer haven than the capital for George VI's children: the future Queen Elizabeth II and her sister Princess Margaret. Today the castle is both a working palace and royal home where the Queen spends many weekends and takes up official residence for several weeks during the Easter period.

ST GEORGE'S CHAPEL

Edward III was born at Windsor Castle and it was he who made the chapel the home of his newly founded Order of the Garter in 1348. In 1475 Edward IV commissioned expansions to St George's Chapel, finally completed in 1528. The first Garter Service since the time of George III was held in 1911 following the investiture of the Prince of Wales, later Edward VIII, and revived again in 1948, 600 years after its founding.

St George's Chapel is the burial place of ten monarchs – Edward IV, Henry VI, Henry VIII, Charles I, George III, George IV, William IV, Edward VII, George V and George VI – and it became the last resting place of the Queen Mother and Princess Margaret following their deaths in 2002.

St George's Chapel is also a venue for royal celebrations, including: the wedding of Prince Edward and Sophie Rhys-Jones in 1999; the service of dedication and prayer following the marriage of Prince Charles to Camilla Parker Bowles in 2005; and the wedding of Prince Harry to Meghan Markle in 2018.

PLACES TO VISIT

Many of the places referred to in *Royal London* are open to visitors.
Please refer to their websites for details of opening days and times.

Banqueting House
www.hrp.org.uk

Buckingham Palace
www.royalcollection.org.uk

Chapel Royal, St James's Palace
www.royal.uk/chapelroyal

Chapels of St John the Evangelist and St Peter ad Vincula
www.thechapelsroyalhmtower
oflondon.org.uk

Clarence House
www.royalcollection.org.uk

Hampton Court Palace
www.hrp.org.uk

Horse Guards Parade
changing-guard.com

Jewel Tower, Westminster
www.english-heritage.org.uk

Kensington Palace
www.hrp.org.uk

Kew Palace
www.hrp.org.uk

Marlborough House
thecommonwealth.org/
marlborough-house

Museum of London
www.museumoflondon.org.uk

National Maritime Museum, Greenwich
www.rmg.co.uk

Old Royal Naval College, Greenwich
www.ornc.org

The Old Vic
www.oldvictheatre.com

Palace of Westminster/ Houses of Parliament
www.parliament.uk

Prince Edward Theatre
www.princeedwardtheatre.
co.uk

Queen's Chapel of the Savoy
royalchapelsavoy.org

The Queen's Gallery
www.royalcollection.org.uk

The Queen's House, Greenwich
www.rmg.co.uk

Royal Botanic Gardens, Kew
www.kew.org

The Royal Exchange
www.theroyalexchange.co.uk

Royal Hospital Chelsea
www.chelsea-pensioners.co.uk

Royal London Hospital Museum
www.bartshealth.nhs.uk/
the-royal-london-hospital-
museum-and-archives

The Royal Mews
www.royalcollection.org.uk

Royal Observatory, Greenwich
www.rmg.co.uk

The Royal Parks
www.royalparks.org.uk

Somerset House
www.somersethouse.org.uk

St Paul's Cathedral
www.stpauls.co.uk

Tower of London
www.hrp.org.uk

Victoria & Albert Museum
www.vam.ac.uk

Westminster Abbey
www.westminster-abbey.org

Windsor Castle and St George's Chapel
www.royalcollection.org.uk